"Fight-Proof Your Marriage" Ed. 1 Released 1/1/2016
© 2015 by Jonathan Hoover. All rights reserved.

Published by J & W Publishers, Derby, KS

No part of this book may be reproduced in any written, electronic, recording, or photocopying without written permission of the publisher or author. The exception would be in the case of brief quotations embodied in the critical articles or reviews and pages where permission is specifically granted by the publisher or author.

Although every precaution has been taken to verify the accuracy of the information contained herein, the author and publisher assume no responsibility for any errors or omissions. No liability is assumed for damages that may result from the use of information contained within.

Scripture quotations marked (NLT) are taken from the Holy Bible, New Living Translation, copyright © 1996, 2004, 2007 by Tyndale House Foundation. Used by permission of Tyndale House Publishers, Inc., Carol Stream, Illinois 60188. All rights reserved.

Scripture quotations marked (NIV) are taken from the Holy Bible, New International Version®, NIV®. Copyright © 1973, 1978, 1984, 2011 by Biblica, Inc.TM Used by permission of Zondervan. All rights reserved worldwide. www.zondervan.com The "NIV" and "New International Version" are trademarks registered in the United States Patent and Trademark Office by Biblica, Inc.TM

This book is not a substitute for the advice of a mental health professional or physician. The reader should regularly consult a physician or therapist in matters relating to his/her health and emotional well-being.

While this book deals with the topic of conflict in marriage relationships, it does not address abusive situations. If you are in a physically abusive relationship, please reach out for help from a trusted source as soon as possible.

FIGHT-PROOF *your* MARRIAGE

Jonathan Hoover

Chapter 1

How We Got to Crazytown

Almost a decade ago, I was a very frustrated, very unhappy young man. My wife and I were in a conflict-filled, stressed-to-the-breaking-point relationship, and I was at the point of desperation. I truly wanted things to be better in our marriage, but I didn't know if that was possible. We fought almost all the time. We were professionals at criticism, blame, defensiveness, name-calling, interrupting, withdrawing, pursuing, and all the other things that make conflict most intense. It seemed we could not have a difficult discussion without it becoming a terrible fight. Keep in mind, neither of us wanted these things for our relationship. We wanted the happy-go-lucky, peace-filled, storybook romance we imagined we'd have when we were dating. But we were stuck with the big ugly truth that we couldn't get along. Now what?

We'd tried a lot of things… we saw a counselor our pastor recommended, but that didn't go well. We tried asking for advice from trusted friends, who loved us, but didn't know how to help. My wife started reading Christian self-help books, and while I wasn't exactly a bookworm, I was thinking about doing some reading myself. This was partly because I truly wanted things to be better, and partly because I didn't want my wife to be able to hold the fact that I'd never read a marriage book over my head. So I went to the local Christian bookstore, found the section labeled "Marriage and Family," grabbed the current best-seller, and opened it with anticipation. Now, I thought, I will learn the secret to making things better.

I read what the author had to say, and felt extremely encouraged. It was as though this writer knew Wendy and me personally, and was able to describe exactly what we were going through. The book talked about all the common things couples do when they get into conflict, and I recognized them as happening in our relationship. In terms of buy-in, I couldn't have been more sold. I was ready for the answers. I knew they would be game-changing in our relationship.

The author then began giving a list of things couples should or shouldn't do in the middle of conflict to make things less contentious. He explained how people shouldn't be critical, call each other by derogatory names, blame each other, say controlling things, withdraw from the conversation, or be sarcastic. Those are only some of his instructions, my memory has faded some since reading the book almost ten years ago. Each of his keys to better conflict made logical sense. I wanted to do better in each of those areas immediately. I wanted to quit saying things that were bound to provoke Wendy to conflict. More importantly, I wanted her to realize she should stop saying those things to me. I quickly vowed never to interrupt again, never to say things in anger, and never to minimize Wendy's feelings.

Armed with our new knowledge gained from reputable marriage books, my wife and I experienced a very short-lived season of contrived peace. We both held our tongues when we were dying to tell each other that we were upset. We worked hard to refrain from calling each other mean names when our blood was boiling. We tried to reverse our pattern of pursuing and withdrawing, even when I was feeling attacked and Wendy was feeling abandoned. Basically, we lived in a strange, alternate reality for a few weeks, desperately trying to achieve the marital harmony the books said was possible.

In those weeks, our relationship didn't get closer, and we eventually buckled under the burden of trying to be something we were not. As a result, we went back to our old, destructive way of dealing with conflict. All those vows I made to be "Mr. Wonderful" during the middle of a fight? Broken. Shattered, actually.

And now, we had a new problem. Now that we were so wonderfully educated about what couples should or shouldn't do in conflict, we had something new to hold over each other's heads. Now we could criticize each other for not following all of the common sense communication rules we read in the books. Now we could tell each other: "You're not doing it right! See, the book says you not supposed to talk to me this way!"

It was such a frustrating season, because everything we read in marriage books about how to deal with conflict made so much sense. It was practical, logical, and reasonable. All of the steps we were supposed to follow to find peace were indisputably good things to do if you want to dismantle tension. We believed in them so much that we memorized them. Yet, we never seemed to be able to follow those instructions long-term. Eventually, we were always back to our old habits of debating and negating each other's feelings, minimizing each other's pain, and ignoring each other's needs.

We eventually hit a breaking point because of all the conflict. I made the decision that I wanted out of our marriage because I felt it was unlikely Wendy and I could ever get along. Fortunately, God most frequently meets us at the point of our brokenness, and guides us toward our destiny. Rather than separate or divorce, my wife and I decided to try couples therapy again, which I believe God used as a tool to save our marriage.

We began to understand each other's needs and relate to each other in better ways. While many couples seem skeptical when I say this, our marriage was transformed from a nearly impossible situation to a close, loving supportive relationship in about six weeks. The nine years since, we've been very close. Today, I'd say we're inseparable.

But back then, even after therapy, we still had an ugly little problem lurking in the closet. While we were doing much better with each other, and fights were much, much rarer, they were still ugly. Sure, we had become better spouses, and we were able to relate to each other in productive, gracious ways when things were going well, but on those occasions when things weren't going well, we proved that we were still pros at pushing each other's buttons.

I joined the staff at NewSpring Church in 2010 as Associate Pastor, and was assigned to coach struggling couples. I really wanted to be good at this. Wendy and I had experienced what it was like to feel very little hope in our relationship. We had also experienced what it was like to have a great counselor help us find the hope we had lost. I desperately wanted to be able to help couples make those same kinds of breakthroughs. So I hit the books. I went back to college and studied to obtain a degree in counseling. I became a voracious reader of Christian marriage books—anything I could find written on the topic. I wanted to be a great marriage coach. But I still knew in the back of my head, that there was one really big problem about which I had very little insight. Conflict.

Sure, I had the books in front of me that said they had all the answers. I once again was staring at all the lists. "Don't criticize your spouse…" one book would say, "try instead to use our word formula to make sure that you don't make them feel attacked." Another resource would say that all men have certain needs, and if those needs aren't met, conflict is bound to be worse. Memorize the list of his needs, make sure you meet them, and then you'll have peace. The same book would then talk about women's needs, so that the husband could respond in kind, making sure to regularly consult the list to make sure he's doing it right. Even a scholarly resource on my shelf (that I deeply respect by the way) gave a list of negative things the researcher had logged while watching couples fight, only to then encourage couples to just "not do them." I felt a sense of deja vu. I'd been here before. I'd read the lists, and I'd tried the word tracks. I'd retrofitted my responses by trying to make sure that everything I said came out right. I'd failed. Frankly, I knew from experience that these lists weren't the answer.

It was all too logical. All the advice, the insight, the lists, the statistics, the charts, the word tracks, they made perfect logical sense. But as a marriage coach, and as a husband, I'd come to the conclusion that people in the middle of conflict aren't logical. They don't say logical things, give logical answers, or respond in logical ways. They are emotional. They express deep feelings in the only way they know how. They are dying to tell the other person what they are truly feeling, but for some reason or other, they can't do it at that moment in a productive way. I began to believe that If logic doesn't drive the train to crazy town, and emotion does, then maybe the answer to conflict won't have much to do with logic, but will have a lot to do with emotion. That was the beginning of the journey that changed my world. I can tell you first-hand that it's been incredibly transformative for Wendy and me, and from what my couples tell me in our coaching ministry, it's been a game changer for them too.

If you've tried logical solutions before but they haven't worked long-term, this book is for you. I've purposely refrained from putting lists of logical "do this" and "don't do this" advice in this book. Instead, I've worked hard to keep this book short, simple, and to the point. I want you to be able to read this text and know how to start changing your relationship for the better right away. And I want you to be able to do that by truly understanding your spouse, not by walking around with a mental checklist of steps to follow.

Keep reading, and you'll see why we lose our minds when we get into fights, why conflict conversations become so personal, and how to get to the real reason for the fight. My hope is that this book will be a journey into freedom for you. When Wendy and I started putting these keys into practice in our relationship, we were able to conquer conflict while still being ourselves. My prayer is that God will use this book to help you reach that place with your spouse as well.

Chapter 2

Losing Our Minds

This, of course, is the premise you've been reading about in the first chapter, but now I'm saying it outright: conflict has the power to make us lose our minds. We probably already realize this intuitively, because we know that when we get into heated conflict we say and do things we later regret. Not only do we regret them, but often we think: *That wasn't me… I don't say things like that… I don't do things like that.* In retrospect, it can almost look like we were acting "crazy" during the fight. And that's not too far from the truth.

Brain science has made huge strides in recent years, helping us understand what's going on in these moments, and while I'm not an expert in behavioral neuroscience, let me try to summarize what happens when we get into these heated discussions.

You're probably already familiar with the idea that fight-or-flight mode is our bodies' physical response to a perceived threat.

And usually, when we think of threatening situations, we imagine physical threats. For instance, if a grizzly bear is chasing you, that's a physically threatening situation, and you're very likely to be triggered into fight-or-flight mode. But consider this for a moment: the majority of threatening situations you face in life are far more likely to be emotionally threatening than physically threatening. You're much more likely to face the threats of rejection, embarrassment, manipulation, control, opposition, mischaracterization, abandonment, and anger (just to name a few) than a grizzly bear. And those emotional threats have just as much potential to trigger us into fight-or-flight mode as physical ones.

When you toggle into fight-or-flight mode, your body changes in a big way. Your pulse quickens, your respiratory rate increases, and your blood pressure spikes. Your digestive system nearly shuts off entirely. Blood is redirected to your limbs (presumably to help you run away from whatever is threatening you), and your entire body gears up to take some sort of action. Our perception becomes very important. Our eyes work harder to produce sharp images, and our physical impulses respond faster. All of this is coordinated by the brain, which acts as the control center for this emergency situation.

In these moments of frantic threat response, the brain processes things and makes decisions differently than it does when you feel calm, cool, and collected. Usually, the decision making center of our brain is the pre-frontal cortex, which serves as the great "processor" of information and decision making. And, when we are functioning in our right minds, the cortex does a wonderful job. It helps us compare situations, analyze the best courses of action for a given situation, understand what is or is not socially acceptable, differentiate good from bad, be flexible, and think abstractly. But when we perceive a major threat, the pre-frontal cortex kind of goes on a mini-vacation, because the reactive "think-first-ask-questions-later" amygdala takes charge.

Along with several other brain changes that take effect during fight-or-flight mode, we become reactive, we think in black and white instead of abstracts, we refuse to think situationally, and instead become very big-picture oriented (this is why it's so easy during a conflict to recall that your spouse also made you feel this way many times before). We react fast, and decisively. With the "parliamentary procedure" of the cortex suspended and the amygdala declaring "martial law," we take swift action, and, at least for the moment, we feel completely sure the action we're taking is the right one.

But then again, in terms of fight-or-flight, this all makes sense. Say you're driving down a two-lane road when you notice an eighteen-wheeler coming from the opposite direction veering into your lane. In that moment, you do not want the pre-frontal cortex to be in charge of your response. It would be too slow. Such a moment is not a time for deep thought. It would not help to try to empathize with the truck driver (i.e. "Gee, I wonder why he's so distracted… maybe he's having a bad day…"). If six tons of steel on wheels is headed directly toward you, it's big picture time. It's time to react—decisively, instinctively, and swiftly. There truly are times when we really need our brain to tell our body to act first and ask questions later. The capacity to respond to threats with reflexive speed could save your life. The problem is that in emotionally threatening situations like marital conflict, fight-or-flight mode can cause us to do some very counterproductive things.

When we find ourselves in fight-or-flight mode in the middle of a conflict we become hypersensitive. Things that our spouse might do or say if we weren't in a fight now become insulting and incendiary. It feels as though there can be no middle ground between our point of view and our spouse's, because we've been sucked into the vortex of black and white thinking. Because abstract thinking isn't available to us in those moments, our ability to empathize with our spouse and truly imagine what it must feel like to be them is not available to us. Simply put, we become absorbed in the content of the conflict to the point that communication breaks down, mutual understanding seems impossible, and we're often behaving quite badly.

No wonder all those wonderful logical conflict resolution techniques we read about in the marriage books don't work in the middle of a fight. We're out of our minds.

It was when my wife and I started learning more about how our brains react to conflict that we realized that we were going to have to re-think everything we'd ever tried before to fix our fights. We were going to have to find a simpler, more direct way to deal with the fight-or-flight reactions we were feeling in the middle of conflict, and it couldn't be complicated. We bought into the idea that *if you can manage to remember one thing during a conflict, you're lucky.* We hadn't even figured out what that one thing was yet. We just knew that was about all we would be capable of… remembering one key to getting out of the fight-or-flight and on to a better place where we could work through our problems. But that "key" would have to be a skeleton key. It would have to work for any fight on any topic. Probably like you, our fights were diverse and could get kind of complex. We needed a way to respond to each other that would cut through the complexity and make resolution possible.

While we were working to figure this out, Wendy and I were stumbling on new things that were really working for us in our own conflict patterns, and I was having great success with the couples I was coaching. We felt like we were almost there… we were dancing around it… and then we stumbled on the idea of the "what and the why."

Chapter 3

The What and the Why

Every once in a while you stumble on a truth that has the power to change the way you see the world. For me, it was one day when I was sitting in a coaching session with a couple who was talking about their marital struggles. As usual, she was telling me all the ways in which he reacts badly in conflict, and he was explaining all the counterproductive ways she handles things. They were both trying to tell me: "They're being unreasonable! Make them be reasonable and quit acting this way."

Also as is usual for one of my coaching sessions, we did a lot of digging. We talked about their past, their family of origin, and their personalities. We talked about past traumatic events and hurts. Eventually, we wound up — the three of us — looking at those "unreasonable" reactions that happen during conflict and viewing them in context with the reasons underneath those reactions, and things started making sense.

Coaches and counselors love patterns, and I was beginning to sense one. I noticed that there was always something *underneath* those rash reactions that happen during conflict. And then the truth that changed my world emerged: ***Underneath every unreasonable reaction is a reasonable pain or fear.*** This idea helped me make sense of the wife who lashes out at her husband, but really just desperately wants to connect with him. It gave me a new view of the husband that yells, because deep down he feels his opinion isn't important to anyone anymore. I bought into this 100%. It changed my coaching ministry. And then it changed our marriage.

6.8 Miles

For some reason, when my body heard the announcement that I had turned thirty, it unaccountably turned against me. I started developing random annoying aches and pains, I started making groaning noises when I got up from a seated position, and I started putting on weight. It's not that I'm a scale-watcher. I've never been one of those people who kept a daily eye on my weight (perhaps that was the problem), but I did notice that over the span of a few short months I had put on well over twenty pounds. This, I was convinced, was a sign of some latent, but significant undiagnosed illness. I went to the doctor and demanded a full workup. I was ready for the worst. I was prepared for the doctor to tell me that I had some rare but dangerous weight-inducing disease. My doctor at the time kind of chuckled and, after giving me a clean bill of health said "I don't think you're sick. You might just be lazy. It's time to do some exercise and dieting. You're over thirty now, and maintaining your old weight will take work." This was not what I wanted to hear, but I had to face the facts. It was time to get healthy. Healthy-ish anyway.

I figured I'd try exercise first. I didn't want to strain myself by both dieting and exercising at the same time. Might as well give them a shot independently. (And yes, this is what my wife has to put up with.) I live in a suburb with plenty of safe sidewalks, so I decided that running was my fastest path to "buff." I decided to get an app for my phone that would track my runs, and, because I didn't look like a goober enough without it, I bought one of those bicep holsters to hold my phone while I shredded those miles.

Speaking of these apps, I quickly learned that they are brutal for your self-esteem. I'm not fiercely competitive, but for some reason this app brought out my obsession for achievement. First of all, it tracks your best times and distances. These are celebrated as "records," and seriously, who doesn't want to set a "record?" Then, I noticed that if I set a "record" I got a badge or a ribbon (albeit a digital one) announcing to the world my superiority over my previous self. I had to have the ribbons. It was a matter of personal pride.

So, whether it was ridiculous or not, I found myself night after night on the sidewalks of my city, desperately pushing myself to set new records. And it was beginning to take a toll. The first few nights of running, I would come home and share my stats with my wife. "Hey babe, I ran 2.5 miles tonight!" She would respond with a genuine smile and a "way to go!" But as I spent the following weeks pushing myself to the limit trying to get yet another of the prized digital badges, she looked less enthusiastic each evening.

One night, I came home glowing (at least I thought I was). I stumbled in the door and proudly announced that I had just completed my best run ever. "Hey babe! I ran 6.8 miles and they were all barely over ten minute miles!" This might not be a huge achievement for a marathon runner, but for me, it was epic, and I expected my wife to jump up, dance in jubilant celebration, throw confetti in the air, and once-and-for-all proclaim me the stud-husband of all time. Instead, she turned toward me with a very disapproving look on her face and said "I'm not impressed by that."

WHAT!?!?!? How could she possibly respond that way? What a hurtful, contentious, disrespectful, and downright mean woman. At least that's what I was thinking at the time. I couldn't believe that she could say such a thing. I stomped off to our master bathroom and took a shower to cool down—both physically and emotionally. I'd like to tell you that my first thought was to try to understand where Wendy was coming from. It wasn't. As I stood in the shower, I was thinking of all the ways I could show Wendy how hurtful her words were to me. I considered giving her the icy-silent-cold-shoulder routine. That was always good for making her pay for her mistakes. Or, I might go the logical route. I could break out one of the dozen or so marriage books I had at the house and show her in black and white why what she did was WRONG, WRONG, WRONG. Or, if I really wanted to make a statement, I could just leave the house for a few hours. I knew that when I just checked out it got her attention. But I couldn't help but feel in that moment that I'd tried all those strategies before, and they always backfired. They hurt Wendy, which in turn hurt me. I needed a new strategy.

I remembered the idea that was working for so many couples I was coaching: underneath every unreasonable reaction is a reasonable pain or fear. As I stood there still fuming, I forced myself to acknowledge that perhaps my wife might have had a reasonable pain or fear underneath her reaction to my run. I replayed her words in my mind, wondering what her reason might be. Then I remembered that my wife had said that 6.8 miles was too much for me. Maybe she was worried about me. I thought. Maybe she thought something bad might happen to me. I wasn't convinced, but it was worth a try. I went upstairs and tried out my theory.

"Were you saying you weren't impressed by my run because you thought I might get hurt or something?" I asked. "Absolutely!" Wendy said. "You come in here looking as though you're about to pass out after running yourself ragged in extreme heat, and it makes me worry you might collapse out there or something. That scares me. You're a great husband and father, and I don't want to lose you." Her response blew me away. What had initially sounded like a huge insult—"I'm not impressed by that"—turned out to be a huge compliment—"I don't want to lose you."

It was such a powerful moment that it led us to the key principle of this book: the what and the why. We believe that every marital conflict or challenge comes pre-packaged with two parts. The first part—the what—is the issue at hand. It's the thing that the conflict appears to be about.

Here are some examples of "what's"

- An annoying habit you wish your spouse would discontinue
- A past sin or poor choice your spouse made
- The way your spouse mishandled a situation
- A big life decision like buying a house or attending college

- The frequency or quality of sex
- The way money is spent
- The way kids are being disciplined or motivated
- Something an in-law did or is doing
- A hurtful comment

And, again, these are just a few examples. "What's" can be anything. A what can be a very minor, innocent thing, like a mistakenly insensitive comment, and they can be a very serious, relationship-ending thing like an affair. Regardless, the "what" is usually the thing that appears to have started the conflict. Talk to a couple in the middle of a fight and ask them what they're fighting about, and they'll usually tell you the "what" of their fight.

Most couples spend the majority of their conflict time hashing and re-hashing the "what's" of their relationship. As a result, they'll never truly get traction. They'll argue with each other, both proving that they don't really care about the other's feelings until they get tired of the fight. Eventually they'll call a truce, and effectively bury the fight in the back yard. But my friends Les and Leslie Parrott always say that buried conflicts have "a high rate of resurrection." Fighting about the "what's" of our relationship was the most tiring, frustrating, and overwhelming part of Wendy's and my relationship. We never really reached resolution, and when we would decide to "call off" the fight, we were merely hitting the "conflict snooze button." The alarm would sound again, only louder next time.

But my work with couples, our little running squirmish, and the idea that reasonable fears lurk underneath unreasonable reactions led us to the belief that underneath every "what" there was something powerful that could unlock the conflict and make resolution possible. It was the skeleton key we had been looking for. We call it the "why." It's the second and much more important part of the conflict. The "why" is the motivation for the fight. It's the emotional push underneath your spouse's unreasonableness. There's a reason why they are upset. Somewhere, deep down, there is pain or fear motivating them to react the way they do, and understanding that reason is the gateway to resolving the conflict.

How do I know that the "why" is better than the "what?" Because the "why" is disarming in a way the "what" can never be. When we're negatively reacting, and activated into fight-or-flight mode, we need to be disarmed. We need some sort of path out of the threatening feelings we experience in the middle of the conflict. What we need to be able to do is find some commonality with the other person. We need to be able to find something we can agree on. After all, an argument is basically two people venting at each other about a topic on which they cannot find common ground. That's what most fights look like. And, for the record, if conflicts were settled by arguing, we wouldn't need judges, juries, or referees, and half the time we don't agree with those people.

Here's what happens with most couples. There are a lot of "what's" in life that they do agree about. They don't fight with each other about those things, because they already have commonality on those topics. But because they're human (read that imperfect), and because spouses come to the relationship with different genders, families of origin, personalities, likes and dislikes, failure points and success strategies, there will be some "what's" where they clash. This is the point of the book where I beg you not to buy into the idea that the way to achieve happiness in a relationship is to debate the "what's" of life until you win your fair share of marital resolutions. If you do that, you'll wear yourself out, and even when you think you've won, you will have lost.

This is the reason the "why" is so important. It's your path to commonality. It's your path to getting on the same page with your spouse. Frankly, it's very unlikely that I will ever believe that 6.8 miles was a dangerous distance for me to run. If the resolution of that conflict had hinged on my acceptance of Wendy's view of the "what," that fight might still be going to this day. But when Wendy told me her "why," I immediately felt commonality with her. When she said, "I don't want to lose you," I identified with that feeling because I don't want to lose her. Regardless of the distance of my run, I wanted her to know that I could identify with her feelings, and that I wanted to understand them better. Not surprisingly, we were done with that fight in a matter of minutes. Actually, because of the very sweet things Wendy meant by what she said, I'd say we grew closer through that conflict. That's very cool. That's ultimately the goal.

How much do I believe this commonality thing works? A lot. Over these past few years, I've told that running story both to couples in my coaching ministry and to large groups. Each time, I get these bewildered looks from the faces of folks when I quote Wendy saying "I'm not impressed by that." The reason they look at me that way is because they can't find common ground with what Wendy said. Then, when I say Wendy complimented me as a husband and father and said she didn't want anything bad to happen to me, I immediately see a look of understanding come over the faces in the room. In an instant, sharing the "why" becomes an "aha moment" for everyone in the room. That's how powerful this is. Imagine the next year of your marriage as a string of "aha moments" that come from discovering the "why's" that motivate your conflict. I'm telling you… this is a game-changer.

Chapter 4

Fighting for the Win

In chapter 5, I'm going to encourage you to "fight for the why." I'm going to give you a clear-cut strategy to use that will help you find that commonality with your spouse we've been talking about in the last chapter. But before we get there, we need to talk about the ways we fight against the "why."

Imagine this… you're at your local hospital being prepared for a major surgical operation. The anesthesiologist activates the drug stream that will send you off to la-la land, as she asks you to count backwards from 100. You float away on a pink cloud, and the operation begins. An hour later, you wake up mid-procedure. You're in intense pain and you expect the surgeon to do something about it… right now. You scream at him to do something. Oblivious, and holding your spleen in his hands, he responds: "Gee, I don't think you're really awake."

It's on now. Before, you were surprised and in pain. Now, you're mad. You start yelling things at the doctor that you wouldn't want your kids or your pastor to hear. You begin insinuating the doctor's medical degree is bogus and that his mom is overweight. One way or the other, you're going to get that doctor to respond—whatever you have to say, whatever you have to do. Then the doctor matter-of-factly says to you: "My therapist told me not to respond to people who talk to me in anger, and your tone of voice is a little out of control right now. I need you to take it down a level or two or I'm not going to dignify anything you said with a response. And in any case, I think I'm a fine surgeon and you're simply a problem patient."

What I've just described for you is the average marital fight in a nutshell. As we've already said, it starts when our spouse experiences personal pain or fear. We might describe that pain in less vulnerable terms by calling it annoyance, frustration, or aggravation, but there's pain or fear at the root. Our spouse expresses that pain to us, but when they do, they don't express it perfectly. This, of course, is normal. Ask a doctor, a dentist, a midwife… people in pain are not usually diplomatic.

Unfortunately, our spouse's less-than-gracious way of expressing themselves often creates in us a reaction of defensiveness ("You're not really awake") or righteous indignation

("My therapist told me not to respond to angry outbursts"). And in the end, it inspires our spouse to believe we won't be there for them. Instead of fighting for the "why," we fight against it. It's not intentional. None of us wake up in the morning planning to prove that we don't care about our spouse's feelings. But in those fight-or-flight moments, we tend to give more pushback than empathy. And in this short chapter we'll talk about the two main things that kill our ability to engage the "why's" in our conflict.

The first way we fight against the "why" is negating. Negating happens when we view the other person's feelings as so unimportant, that we reject or minimize them. It's basically the same thing as saying, "This may be important to you, but it's a non-issue to me." Maybe we feel like their viewpoint is so invalid that it doesn't even deserve a response. Perhaps we feel that they are making too big a deal out of an issue, and we try to get them to "chill out." Either way, we're sending the message that we don't care about their fear or pain, and that we're not going to do anything about it. This is what happens when the surgeon tells the patient, "I don't think you're really awake." The problem, of course, with negating is that it makes the other person feel completely unheard. Worse, it makes them feel that you won't be there for them when they need you most. It is this negating dynamic that so often creates desperation in couples. This is when the fight-or-flight response becomes turbo-charged.

The second way we fight the "why" is debating. We debate when we feel like the issue is important, but our spouse is wrong. This, of course, is the classic way arguments start. Two people find themselves with two very different viewpoints about an issue they both deem important, and they try to find convincing ways to win over their opponent. The object is to walk away from the interaction with the firm knowledge that you convinced the other person that they are wrong, and you are right. But every time you win an argument you lose closeness in your relationship.

While I'm on the subject of arguments, let me just assure you that in marriage, they are a total waste of time. Psychologists refer to something called "confirmation bias" that proves the pointlessness of arguing. Confirmation bias tells us that our brains are most likely to pay attention to evidence that proves what we already believe to be true, and they tend to ignore or reject evidence that disconfirms our beliefs. So then, I think we can safely say that two people trying to debate with each other, presenting evidence that disconfirms each other's beliefs, are very likely to get nowhere.

Here, we can benefit from what the Bible teaches in the book of Ecclesiastes:

Ecclesiastes 7:20 (NIV)
20 Indeed, there is no one on earth who is righteous,
no one who does what is right and never sins.

We tend to debate with our spouse because we believe we are right. Our brains are paying attention to evidence that seems to prove we are right, and the fight-or-flight response is telling us to go with our gut. Unfortunately, we're not perfect, and often we are not right. Ultimately, no one is there to referee our marriage and decide who has the most accurate viewpoint. This means that if we want to get past the habits of debating and negating, we must ultimately decide to worry less about who's right, and worry more about how to connect.

If you think you've slipped into the habits of debating and negating with your spouse, don't be discouraged. We all tend to do these things. The key is to grasp the fact that these strategies for dealing with conflict not only don't work, but are also robbing you of your capacity to get to the "why's" that could help you find common ground with your spouse. In the next chapter, I'll give you one very basic strategy for finding the "why's" in your marriage.

Chapter 5

Fighting For the Why

When I share the idea of fighting for the "why" with couples, one of the most frequent responses I get is, "We already do that. We ask each other 'why' questions during a fight, and it only makes things worse."

Usually, by this they mean that they ask questions like:

- Why do you always have to be so stubborn?
- Why can't you be there at one of the kids' ball games?
- Why did you forget my birthday?
- Why can't you open up and talk?
- Why can't you shut up?
- Why can't you let me have my space when we're upset with each other?
- Why can't you stay here and talk to me when we're upset with each other?
- Why don't you like my parents?

- Why can't you see that it's time to sell this house and buy a new one?

While the word "why" is indeed in these questions, they are very likely doomed to failure. They are guaranteed to inspire the other person to become defensive. That's the last thing we want. Keep in mind that in asking for the "why," you're inviting the other person to teach you something about them, not defend themselves. You're inviting them to be vulnerable—asking them to look deep into their heart and think about why they've reacted negatively to something. You're not putting them on the defense stand, interrogating them under oath about their motive for the "crime" they committed. If you find yourself playing that part—the part of the prosecutor, your "why" questions will always sound like attacks. Instead, you want to be the defense attorney—the person who asks questions because you earnestly want to understand.

Since I'm admitting that this can be tricky, and since I promised from the beginning to make dismantling marital conflict simple, I'm going to give you a pre-worded question you can ask your spouse that will help you get to the "why" without making them feel attacked. I admit, I'm not much for word tracks, because I feel the best communication in marriage comes from the heart, but this is one question that is best asked a certain way.

Fighting For the Why

Here's that question:
What is it that bothers you so much about this?

There are three reasons why this question works when others don't. First, it encourages the other person to explain their reaction, instead of defend their position. After all, it was the other person's unreasonable reaction that caused this to be a fight instead of a discussion. We each have the capacity to discuss a difference of opinion with anyone—even our spouses. Discussions turn into fights because of unreasonable reactions. And, as we've said before, those unreasonable reactions are the warning lights that let us know somewhere under the hood there is a reasonable pain or fear. The goal, then of any "why" question should be to understand the reaction. This, we have already said, is the way to find commonality and move forward.

The second reason this question works is that it has been engineered to be a least common denominator question. Notice that we use the word "bother" instead of having you make guesses about the emotion the other person is feeling. For example, we could have encouraged you to ask: "What is it about this that makes you so angry?" But the other person might not be feeling angry, and if you guess wrong, they are very likely to shut you down fast, because they will feel you don't really understand them. Instead, we use the word "bother" because it encompasses so many potential emotions. Asking this question helps the other person know that you've noticed a negative reaction to something on their part, and that they appear to be "bothered." You're inviting them to share the reason why with you, and in so doing, you're offering to empathize with them and be their advocate.

Finally, and potentially most importantly, this question gives you an escape sequence from a debate. Remember that we've said a debate is all about the "fight to be right." With a small retrofit, we can use this powerful question to escape any argument you happen to be in. I'll show you how.

Imagine my wife comes to me and says,
"Jonathan, you're the laziest man on the face of planet earth."

When she says this, I can think of at least one lazier person than I, so I get ready to strike back with,
"No I'm not!"

Of course, in saying that, I've completed the debate loop, and Wendy and I will cycle around in a childish "yes you are/no you're not" back and forth until we both wear each other out. Instead, imagine if I were to respond this way:
"Suppose you're right—what bothers you so much about that?"

By saying "suppose you're right," I'm skipping past the question of who has the "correct" view of this situation, and I'm inviting her to share her real feelings.

What we learn from the "what and why" concept that I've shared so far in this book is that every fight involves two messages from your spouse. The first message is what they're actually telling you. The second message is what they're dying to tell you. The "what" is usually the message that is coming out of your spouse's mouth. Don't be surprised if it includes exaggeration, extremism, and hyperbole. These are all signs that underneath the "what" they're sharing with you is a powerful "why" that they're dying to let out. They just don't know how. They're struggling to get the real, vulnerable truth about their fear or pain out in the open. By asking them, "What bothers you so much about this?", you're inviting them to go to that vulnerable place and let their true feelings out.

Just beware, this question will not automatically and instantly soften the anger or upset the other person is feeling. Usually, it will not "talk them off the ledge" immediately. That means that the very first time you ask, "What is it about this that bothers you so much?" in the conversation, you might get it thrown right back in your face. The key is to stick with it. Here's what I mean by this. Imagine we toggle back to that conversation where Wendy accused me of being the laziest person in the world.

We'll take a look at the way the dialogue might go if this fight were typical for an average couple:

> *Two things about the dialogue you're about to read… first, it never happened. Wendy is much kinder to me than this little hypothetical example makes her sound. Secondly, we used a little retrofit to that question we've been talking about. When in an argument, try adding the phrase "suppose you're right…" to the beginning. This gives you an off-ramp for that "fight-to-be-right" loop, and allows you to start addressing the real issues.*

Wendy: Jonathan, you are the laziest man on planet earth!

Jonathan: Suppose you're right; what bothers you so much about that?

Wendy: What bothers me about that?!? Of course it bothers me because it means you're a jerk!

Jonathan: Okay, suppose you're right that I'm a jerk; what bothers you so much about that?

Wendy: Anyone would be bothered by being married to a jerk.

Jonathan: Okay, suppose you're right about everything you've said up until now and I'm a lazy jerk; what bothers you so much about that?

Wendy starts to soften, slow down her response, and looks as though she's thinking things through. At some point, a deep breath happens.

Wendy: (Still kind of mad) It means that I can't count on you when I need you.

Jonathan: Suppose you're right that you can't count on me; what bothers you so much about that?

Wendy: I guess it bothers me because I'm overwhelmed at the prospect of handling all of the tasks in my life without your help. I feel like I can't do it on my own.

This, of course, is where you hit pay dirt. At some point during your journey to find the "why," you'll watch that other person sort of back away from the ledge, calm down a little bit, take a deep breath, think things through and start talking to you about what's really underneath their unreasonable comments or reaction. I've used this technique with many couples in my office, and I can vouch for the fact that no matter how emotional a person might seem, or how stoic, we all have something we're dying to communicate deep inside. Using this question helps you open the doorway to that powerful and transcendent conversation. So don't give up the first time that your spouse doesn't immediately melt when you ask for the "why." Stay with it; help them see that you really do care.

Often in my marriage ministry, I sit across from a man or woman who assures me that their spouse cannot be pleased. No matter what they do, they seem to somehow make their spouse mad, and they are tired of the random fights that spring up for "no reason at all." They often feel that living with their spouse is like walking through a mine field. They have no idea where to step without getting "blown up." Here, fighting for the why can be a truly liberating experience. If you try to make sense of your fights by only looking at the "what's" that prompt them, at best, you'll end up with a list of topics to be avoided. And as I've said in my book "The Blindfolded Marriage," the topic of avoidance can end up being the beginning of trust breakage. If, however, you choose to think through the "why's" underneath your fights, you'll begin to see a grid that becomes a map for the mine field. By this, I mean that, at the deepest levels, most of us only have a few "why's." This is true of your spouse. They very likely only have a few key things that motivate the unreasonableness. Once you understand those, it all begins to make more sense.

Fighting For the Why

In the last chapter, we'll talk about what to do with the "why" once you have it.

Chapter 6

What to Do with the Why

I truly believe that getting to the "why" without debating or negating is 90% of the battle in defeating conflict. If you achieve this, you will be far ahead of the curve. And, to a certain extent, the answer to the question "What do we do when we get to the why?" is "You'll know." I say this, because you very likely have all the skills to handle this naturally. I feel certain you have intelligence, compassion, empathy, and the capacity to understand and care about another person's feelings. The issue is that all these wonderful qualities don't tend to surface when we're focused on the "what" and not the "why." But that's done now. Moving forward, you're a "why"-finding machine. And when you find those "why's," I'll wager you shock yourself with how well you handle working through them.

However, I will make a couple of comments here about how to respond to the "why" when it surfaces. First, it's important to say that you don't have to agree with your spouse's "why," but you do have to respect it. By this, I mean that if your spouse's "why" is: "I feel like you won't be there for me when I need you most," you obviously don't have to agree with them (Saying something like: "You're right. I won't be there for you"). But on the other hand, you don't want to flip back into debating or negating (Saying something like: "That's ridiculous"). Your spouse's "why" is important to them whether or not you think it's wholly accurate. Remember, the "why" is a path you follow to commonality… but following that path is your choice. You can either slap the "why" away by disrespecting it, or you can welcome it as a chance to move forward.

And before I leave the topic of respect, It wouldn't hurt for us to take a quick look at God's instructions for marriage in Ephesians chapter five.

> *Ephesians 5:21 (NLT)*
> *21 And further, submit to one another out of reverence for Christ.*

The word rendered "submit" in this verse basically means to put the other person first. And the reason we should do this, according to the verse, is because of our "reverence for Christ." This means that our willingness to respect our spouse's "why's" shouldn't be based on their performance, their perfection, their reasonableness, their fairness, or their willingness to return the favor, but on our respect for God. That's a pretty massive thought to digest. By the way, notice that this verse doesn't say that your "why's" don't matter. Putting your spouse first doesn't mean that you are expected to forget yourself in the process. You still have feelings, and they matter. It's just that success demands a willingness to push your spouse's needs to the front of the line. A marriage with two people screaming "Me First!" has no hope.

The one last thing I'd like to mention here is that one of the greatest things you can do to help the conflict dynamic in your marriage along with learning how to find your spouse's "why" is learning how to find your own "why" when you feel activated. Some time ago, I was doing something called Intensive Marital Coaching with couples where they would come in for an all-day session. All-day sessions were very interesting. Often, at some point during the day, the couple would end up in a fight in my office; sometimes they were very intense fights. When that would happen, I would invite the couple to take a break, and I gave each of them something I call the Excavation Worksheet. Actually, it doesn't deserve to be called a worksheet because it only consists of two half-sentences that I want them to finish.

Here are the sentences:

What hurts the most right now is…

_____.

What I'm most afraid of right now is…

_____.

Sound familiar? Underneath every unreasonable reaction is a reasonable pain or fear. Almost without fail, about a minute after the couple started writing on their worksheets, I would hear one or both of them take a deep breath in, and a deep breath out. That deep breath was a beautiful thing. It's a sign that the brain is finding its way out of fight-or-flight mode, and that some sanity is creeping back into the thought stream. That's how powerful finding your own "why" can be. Even if your spouse isn't interested in figuring out what's motivating your unreasonable reactions, you should be. Most of us react out of habit and instinct, not out of a clear sense of our deepest hurts and fears. We need to be in touch with those motivators if we want to learn how to direct our emotional energies well. Try this, and see for yourself how powerful it can be. If you would like to get the actual worksheet, you can download it from my blog at www.lifeinacrazyworld.com.

In Conclusion

I would like to tell you that as soon as Wendy and I discovered this "what" and "why" thing that we immediately implemented it in our conflict and never had a hurtful fight ever again, but that isn't how it worked for us. I think now from experience in our coaching ministry we can say it doesn't seem to be how it works for most people.

When we first worked on this, we still had our same old fights—they happened the same old way and they were full of the same old useless, unproductive patterns. But after the fight was over and we had both calmed down, one or both of us would come back to the other and we'd say something like, "We forgot to do that "why" thing…" and we'd get to the "why" after the fact (that is still a victory, by the way).

Then, as we progressed, we would be in the middle of a fight with our same old habits when one of us would realize that we needed to stop and talk about the "why." When you start doing that, you've reached a powerful stage, because you're starting to break the old pattern. A great way to say this is, "Time out! We haven't talked about the why." After you do this for a little while, there will come a day… a glorious, wonderful, fantastic day when you will be in the middle of a discussion with your spouse about both of your feelings, and concerns and you'll think to yourself, We did it… We skipped the fight! We went right to the important stuff! When that happens, my friend, throw a party. You managed to fight-proof your marriage.

I pray God's richest blessings on you and your relationship. May you grow close to Christ together and experience his best in your relationship.

Acknowledgements

This book would never have been possible without my precious wife, Wendy. Her input and wisdom impacted every page. Were it not for her willingness to read my drafts, share ideas and insight, and catch my many typos, this book never would have happened.

I also would like to thank my friend, Dr. Ryan Schroeder. He is a tremendously talented neuropsychologist. His input was priceless as I was exploring the idea of how fight-or-flight mode impacts conflict.